# Rabbits

by Helen Frost

Consulting Editor: Gail Saunders-Smith, Ph.D.

Consultant: Jennifer Zablotny, D.V.M.,
Member, American Animal Hospital Association

## Pebble Books

an imprint of Capstone Press
Mankato, Minnesota

Pebble Books are published by Capstone Press
151 Good Counsel Drive, P.O. Box 669, Mankato, Minnesota 56002
http://www.capstone-press.com

1 2 3 4 5 6 06 05 04 03 02 01

*Library of Congress Cataloging-in-Publication Data*
Frost, Helen, 1949–
    Rabbits/by Helen Frost.
    p. cm.—(All about pets)
    Includes bibliographical references and index.
    Summary: Simple text and photographs present the features and care of rabbits.
    ISBN 0-7368-0659-8
    1. Rabbits—Juvenile literature. [1. Rabbits as pets. 2. Pets.] I. Title. II. All about
pets (Mankato, Minn.)
SF453.2 .F76 2001
636.9'322—dc21

00-022985

## Note to Parents and Teachers

The All About Pets series supports national science standards for
units on the diversity and unity of life. This book describes domesti-
cated rabbits and illustrates what they need from their owners. The
photographs support emergent readers in understanding the text.
The repetition of words and phrases helps emergent readers learn
new words. This book also introduces emergent readers to subject-
specific vocabulary words, which are defined in the Words to Know
section. Emergent readers may need assistance to read some words
and to use the Table of Contents, Words to Know, Read More,
Internet Sites, and Index/Word List sections of the book.

# Table of Contents

Pet Rabbits . . . . . . . . . . . . . . 5
How Rabbits Look. . . . . . . . . . 7
What Rabbits Need. . . . . . . . 15

Words to Know . . . . . . . . . . 22
Read More . . . . . . . . . . . . . 23
Internet Sites. . . . . . . . . . . . 23
Index/Word List. . . . . . . . . . 24

Some rabbits are pets.

Rabbits have long ears.

Rabbits have whiskers.

Rabbits have strong legs.

Rabbits have soft fur.

Rabbits need a hutch.

Rabbits need
food and water.

Rabbits need hay.

Rabbits need
a place to play.

# Words to Know

**food**—something that people, animals, and plants need to stay alive and grow; rabbits eat rabbit food pellets, hay, and some fruits and vegetables.

**fur**—the soft, thick, hairy coat of an animal; the fur of rabbits can be white, gray, black, or brown.

**hay**—dried grass; rabbits need to eat hay to stay healthy.

**hutch**—a pen or coop for small pets; rabbits need a hutch that is big enough for them to move around; rabbit hutches may be indoors or outdoors.

**pet**—a tame animal kept for company or pleasure; only certain kinds of rabbits should be kept as pets; wild rabbits do not make good pets.

**whisker**—one of the long, stiff hairs near the mouth of some animals; rabbits use whiskers to feel.

# Read More

**Evans, Mark.** *Rabbit.* ASPCA Pet Care Guides for Kids. New York: Dorling Kindersley, 1992.

**Schaefer, Lola.** *Family Pets.* Families. Mankato, Minn.: Pebble Books, 1999.

**Spangard, Kristine.** *My Pet Rabbit.* All About Pets. Minneapolis: Lerner Publications, 1997.

**Vrbova, Zuza.** *Rabbits.* Junior Pet Care. Broomall, Penn.: Chelsea House, 1997.

# Internet Sites

**Critter Collection: Rabbits**
http://animalnetwork.com/critters/profiles/rabbit/default.asp

**House Rabbit Society**
http://www.rabbit.org

**Pet Care**
http://www.aspca.org/learn/petcare.html

# Index/Word List

are, 5
ears, 7
food, 17
fur, 13
have, 7, 9, 11, 13
hay, 19
hutch, 15
legs, 11
long, 7

need, 15, 17, 19, 21
pets, 5
place, 21
play, 21
soft, 13
some, 5
strong, 11
water, 17
whiskers, 9

## Word Count: 37
## Early-Intervention Level: 3

**Editorial Credits**

Martha E. H. Rustad, editor; Linda Clavel, designer; Jodi Theisen and Katy Kudela, photo researchers; Crystal Graf, photo editor

**Photo Credits**

Gregg Andersen, cover
Norvia Behling, 1, 10, 18
Photo Network/Tom McCarthy, 4
Unicorn Stock Photos/Dick Keen, 6; Chris Boylan, 12; Andre Jenny, 14; Martha McBride, 20
Visuals Unlimited, 16; Visuals Unlimited/S. Strickland—Naturescapes, 8

Special thanks to Pet Expo in Mankato, Minnesota, for their help with photo shoots. The author thanks the children's section staff at the Allen County Public Library in Fort Wayne, Indiana, for research assistance. The author also thanks Nancy T. Whitesell, D.V.M., at St. Joseph Animal Hospital in Fort Wayne, Indiana.